Life Is A Rollercoaster
& 9 more chart hit

GW00602068

CONTENTS

Dancing In The Moonlight	Toploader	2
Dirty Water	Made In London	6
Fill Me In	Craig David	12
Genie In A Bottle	Christina Aguilera	18
Life Is A Rollercoaster	Ronan Keating	23
If Only	Hanson	28
Life Story	Angie Stone	34
Sex Bomb	Tom Jones & Mousse T	38
Sitting Down Here	Lene Marlin	44
So Long	Fierce	50

Production: Anna Joyce

Published 2000

International Music Publications Limited
Griffin House 161 Hammersmith Road London W6 8BS England

DON'T BE
A MUSIC
COPYCAT!

The copying of © copyright
material is a criminal offence
and may lead to prosecution

Dancing In The Moonlight

Words and Music by
SHERMAN KELLY

Dirty Water

Words & Music by
PETER IBSEN, KELLY BRYANT, MARIANNE MELHUS, MELISSA POPO,
SHERENE DYER, MIKE STEER AND SACHA SKARBEK

1. I nev-er thought that you could be that way.
2. As e-vil thoughts dwell in your soul.

Friends from young and now you've changed.
Grinding your mind into a hole.

Love and trust has turned to hate.
filled with spite and ten - sion.

If I'd have known you'd do me ov - er.
You give me no - thin' but de - cep - tion.

De -
What's

Fill Me In

Words and Music by
CRAIG DAVID AND MARK HILL

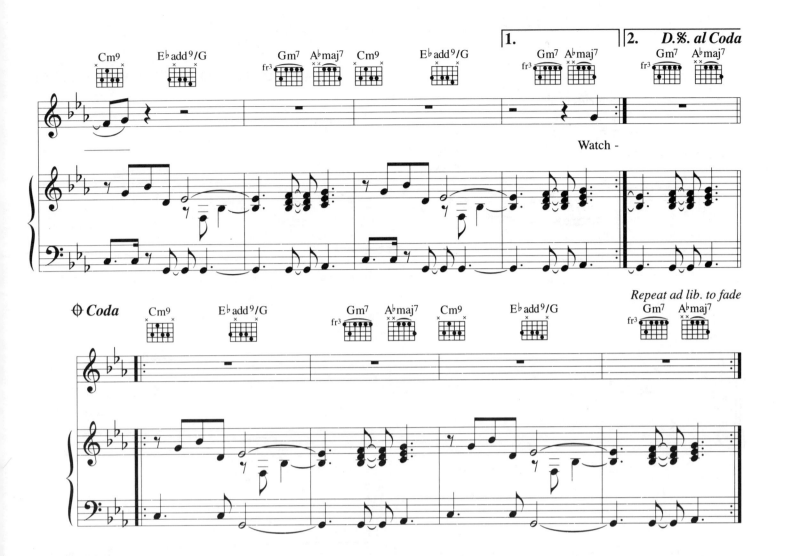

Watch -

Verse 2:
Whenever the coast was clear and she'd ask me to come out
I'd say "Hey girl, come on right around"
So she knocked at the door
I was standing with the keys in my hand to the four-by-four
Jumped in my ride checking that nobody saw
The club we went in, we got down
Bounce, bounce to the rhythm
Saw it was early morning
Thought we'd better be leaving
So I gave you my jacket for you to hold
Told you to wear it cos you felt cold
I mean me and her didn't mean to break the rules
I wasn't trying to play your mum and dad for fools
We were just doing things young people in love do
Parents trying to find out what we were up to.

Saying why can't you keep your promises no more
Saying you'll be home by twelve, come strolling in at four
Out with your girls, but leaving with the boy next door
Can you fill me in? (fill me in)
Wearing a jacket who's property
Said you'd been queuing for a taxi
But you left all your money on the TV (you tell 'em, babe)
Can you fill me in? (can you fill me in).

Genie In A Bottle

Words and Music by
PAM SHEYNE, DAVID FRANK AND STEVE KIPNER

Life Is A Rollercoaster

Words and Music by
RICK NOWELS AND GREGG ALEXANDER

If Only

Words and Music by
ISAAC HANSON, TAYLOR HANSON AND ZACHARY HANSON

Life Story

Words and Music by
GERRY DEVEAUX AND CRAIG ROSS

There ain't no oth - er way for us___ than love.___

Guitar

'Cause this is

D.%. Repeat Chorus ad lib. to fade

Sex Bomb

Words and Music by
MOUSSE T AND ERROL RENNALLS

Sitting Down Here

Words and Music by
LENE MARLIN

So Long

Words and Music by
ANDREA MARTIN, CAMUS CELLI AND ANDRES LEVIN

Printed in England
The Panda Group · Haverhill · Suffolk · 8/00